MOST OF ALL

―――――――――――

WRITTEN BY:

―――――――――――

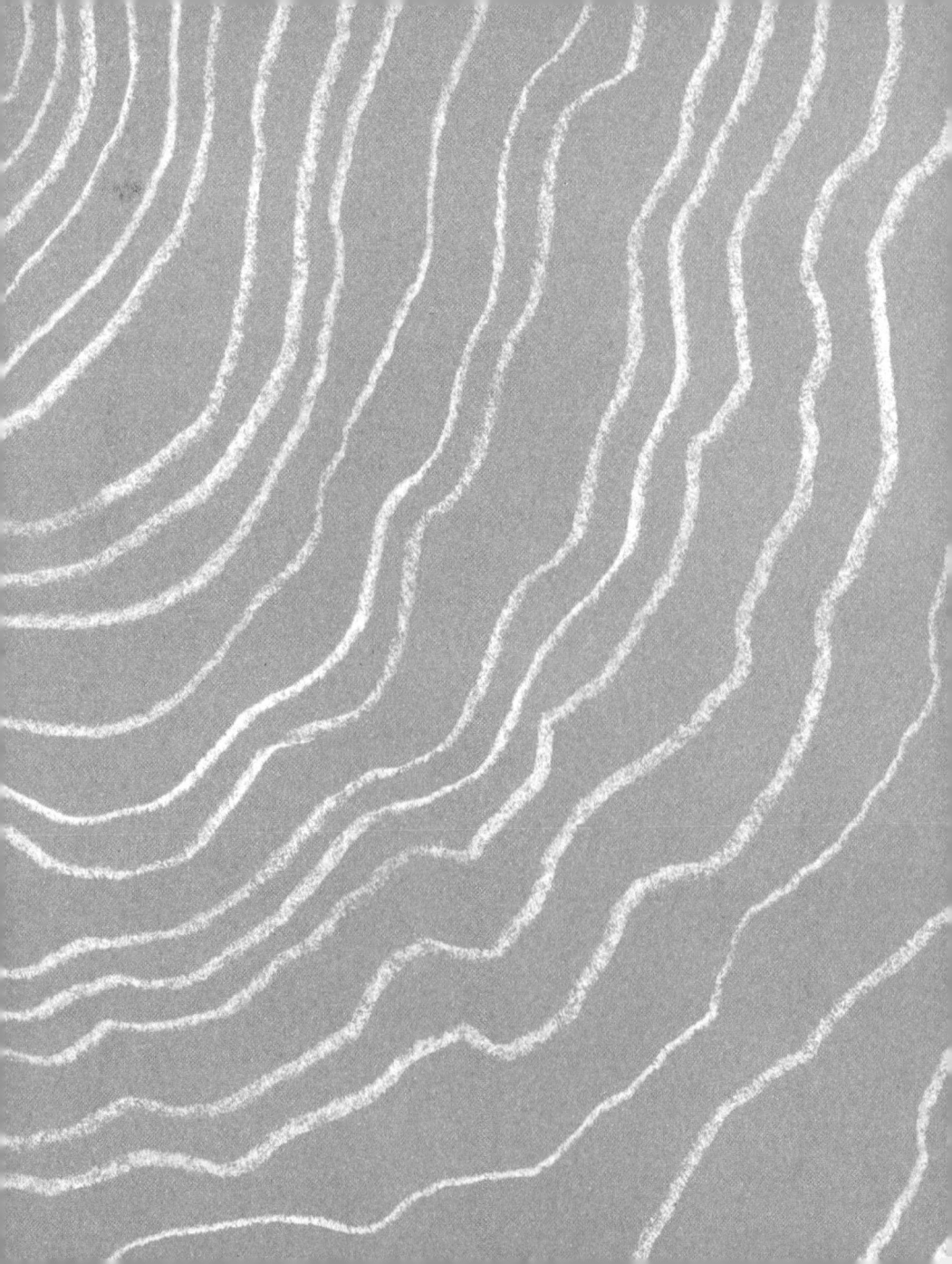

This is a place for a lifetime of wisdom.

It's a place for understanding, a place for perspective, a place to hold the thoughts of one person very close.

Because one person touches many. Because stories can travel across time. Because love knows no distance at all.

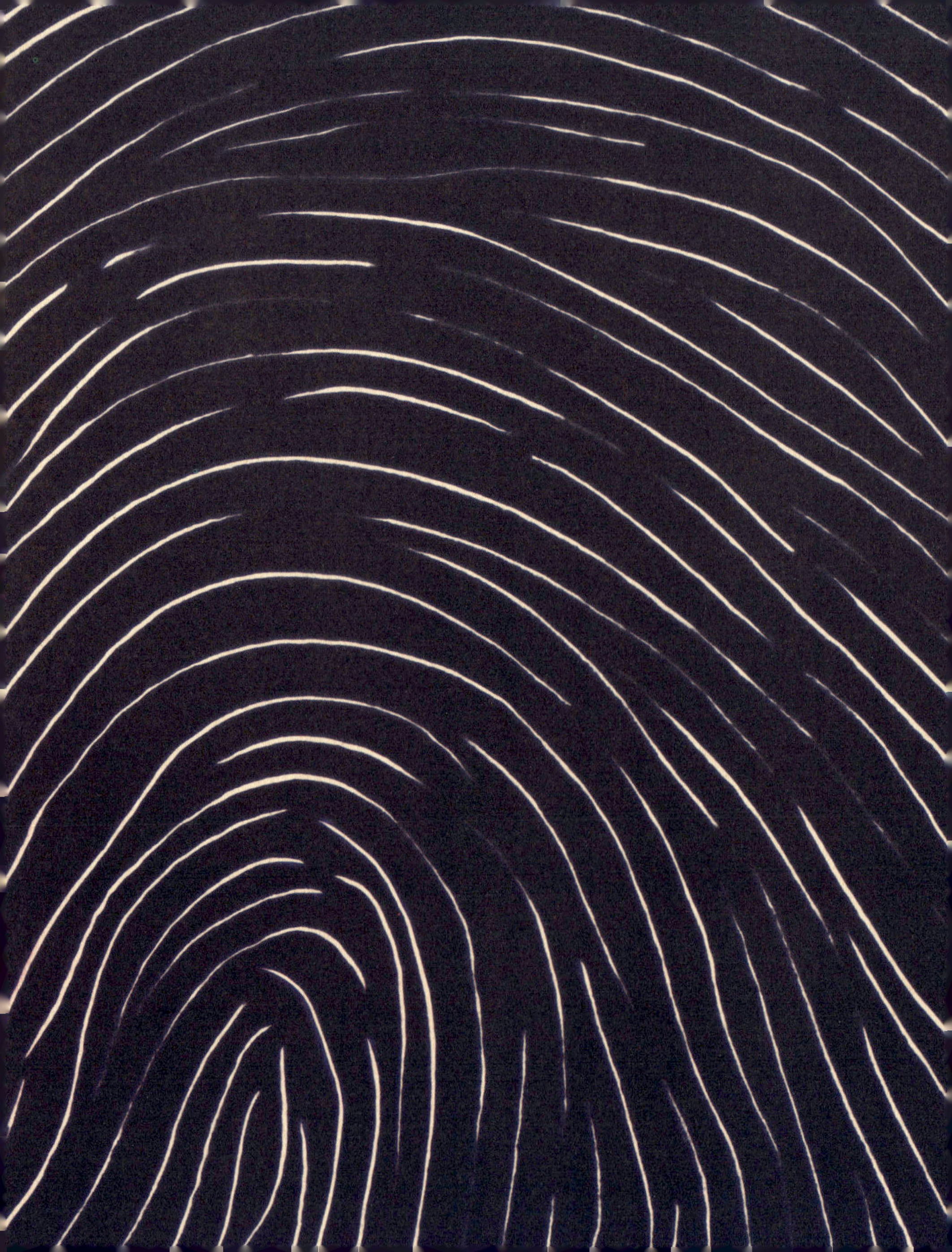

The older I've gotten, the more
I've come to believe that:

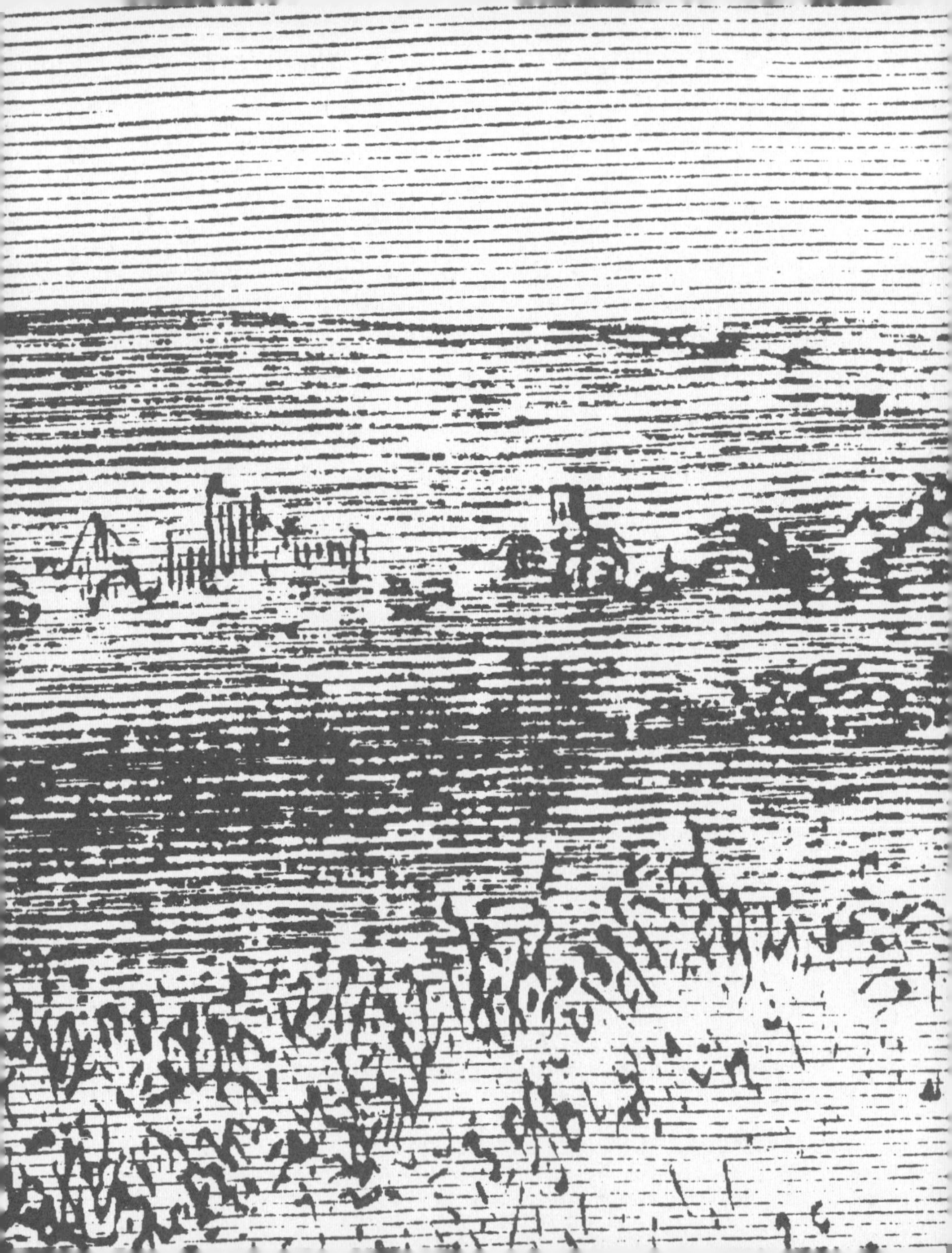

If I could ask everyone in the world
to do one thing, it would be this:
_____

_____

_____

_____

_____

I think if people did,
the world would be:
_____

_____

_____

_____

_____

_____

_____

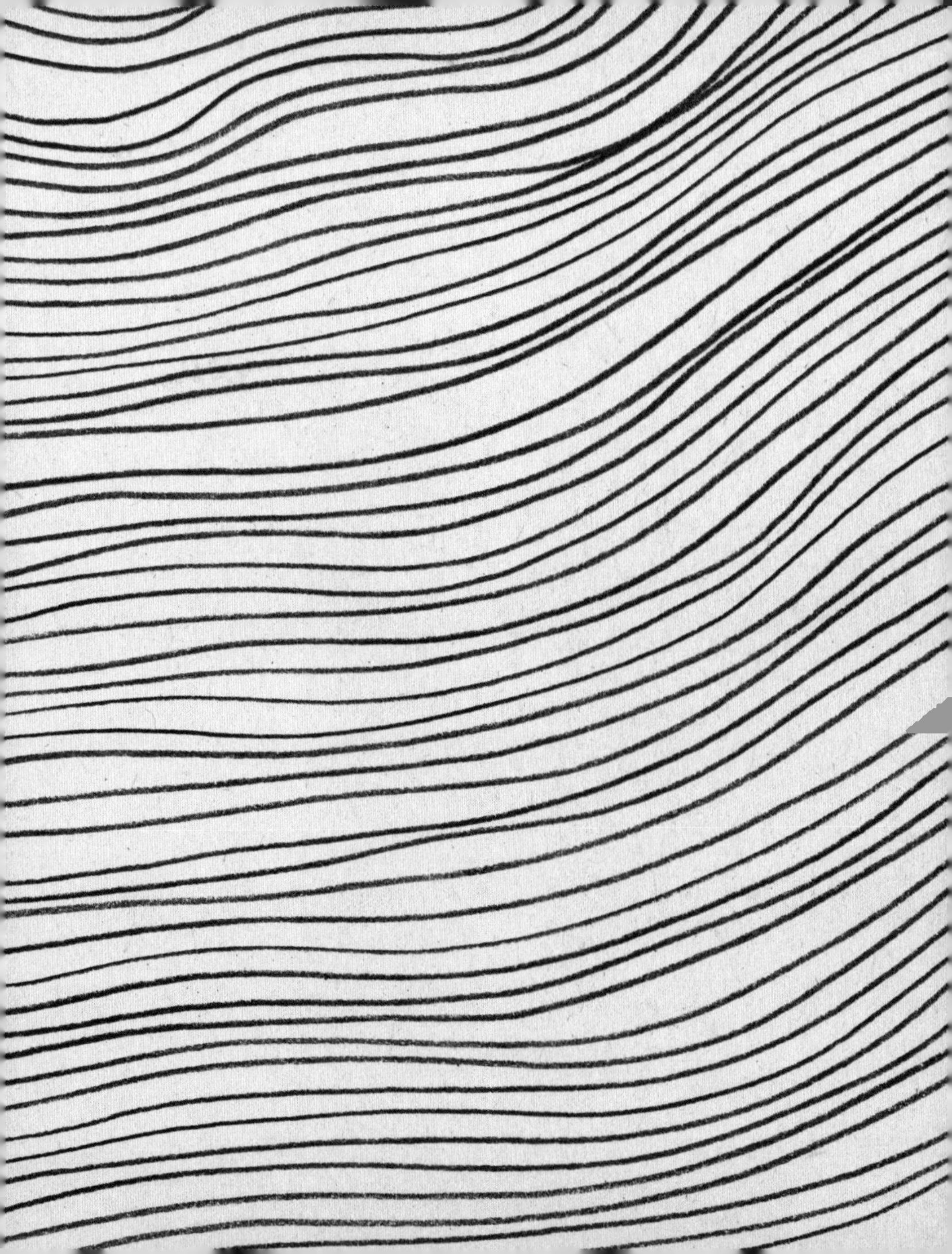

IT SEEMS
LIKE THE DAYS
I MAKE TIME TO

_____

AND

_____

ARE ALWAYS
GOOD DAYS.

...becoming
isn't about arriving
somewhere... the
journey doesn't end.

MICHELLE OBAMA

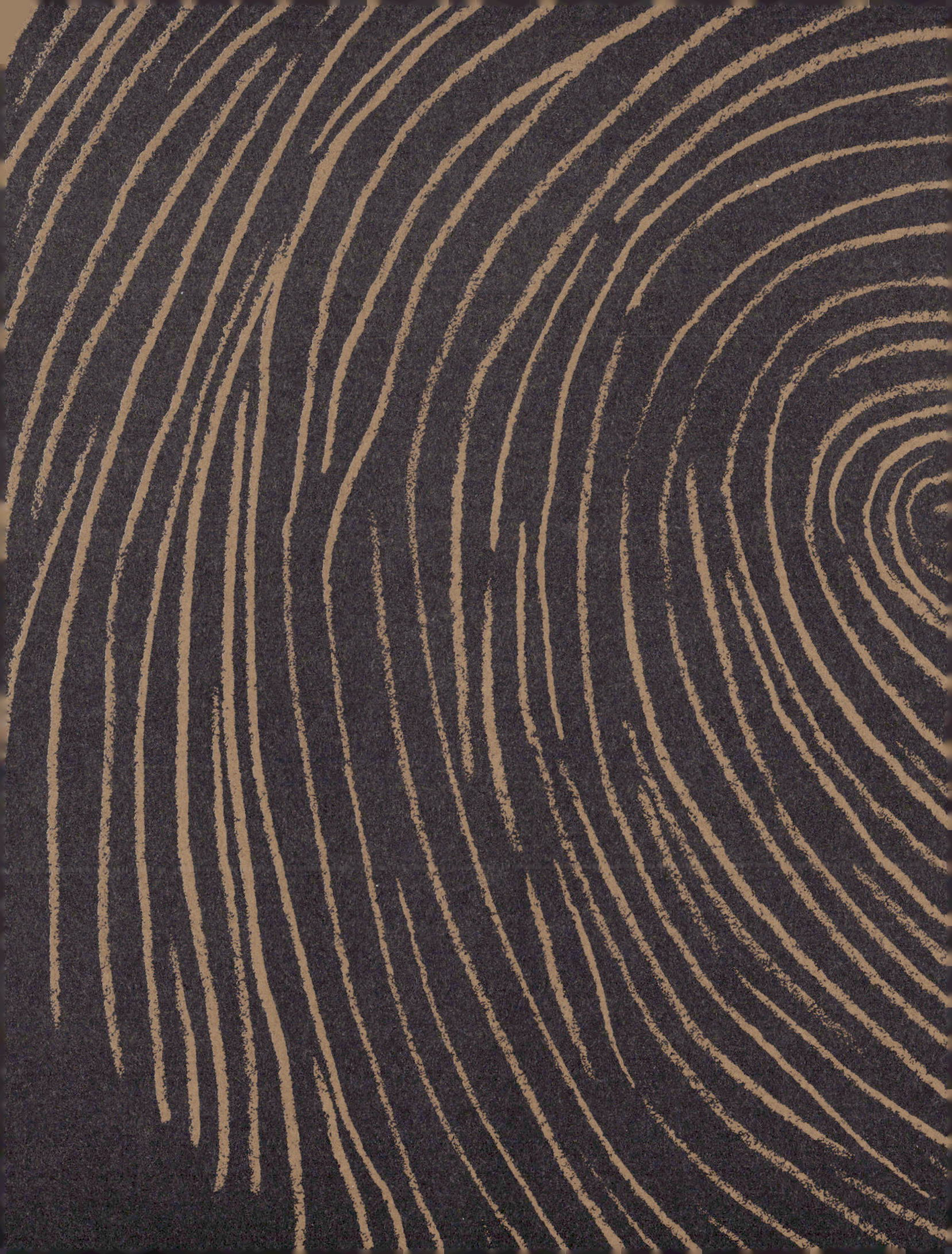

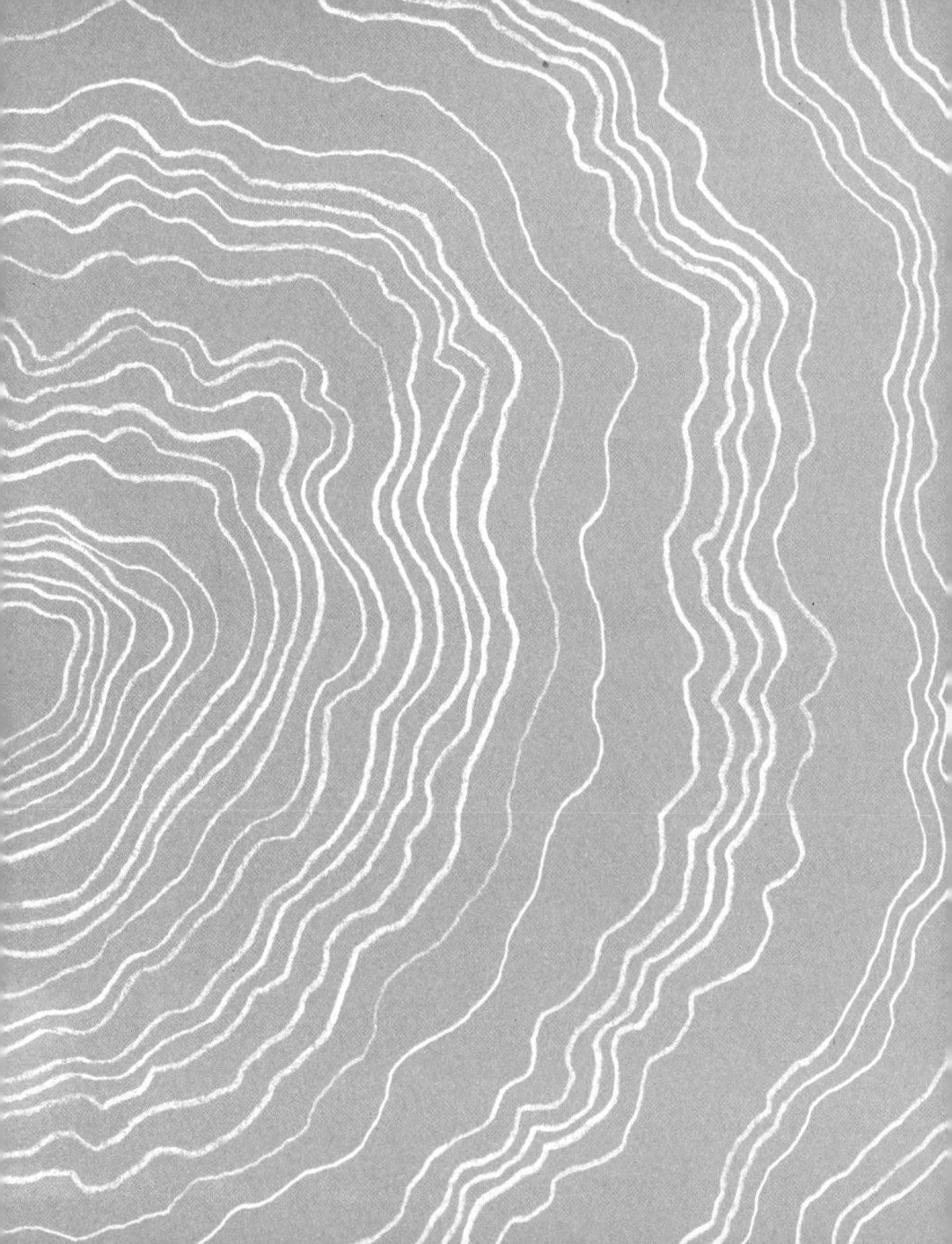

One of the biggest accomplishments
of my life was learning how to:

Here's how it changed me:

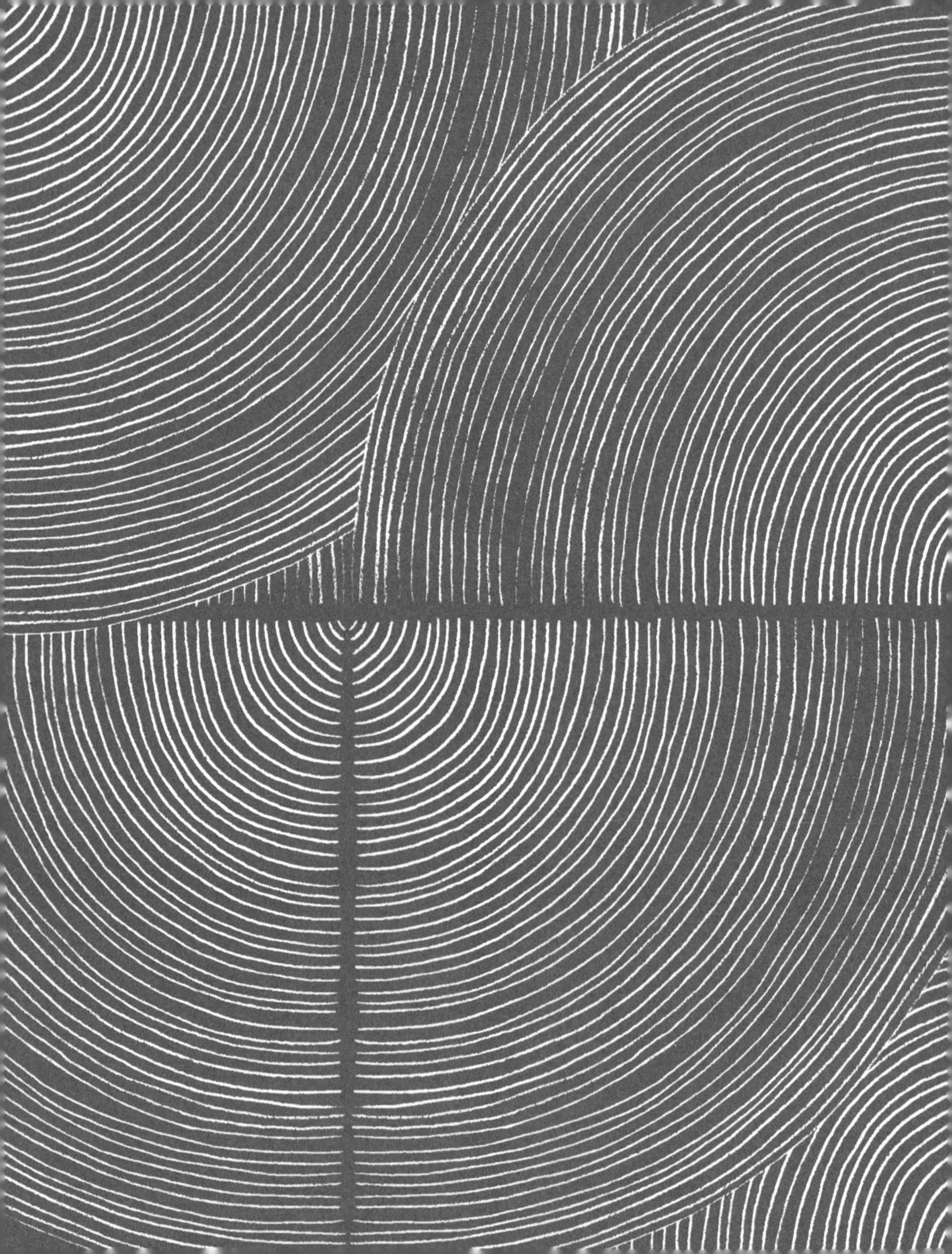

This is something I learned the hard way:

And here's what that experience taught me:

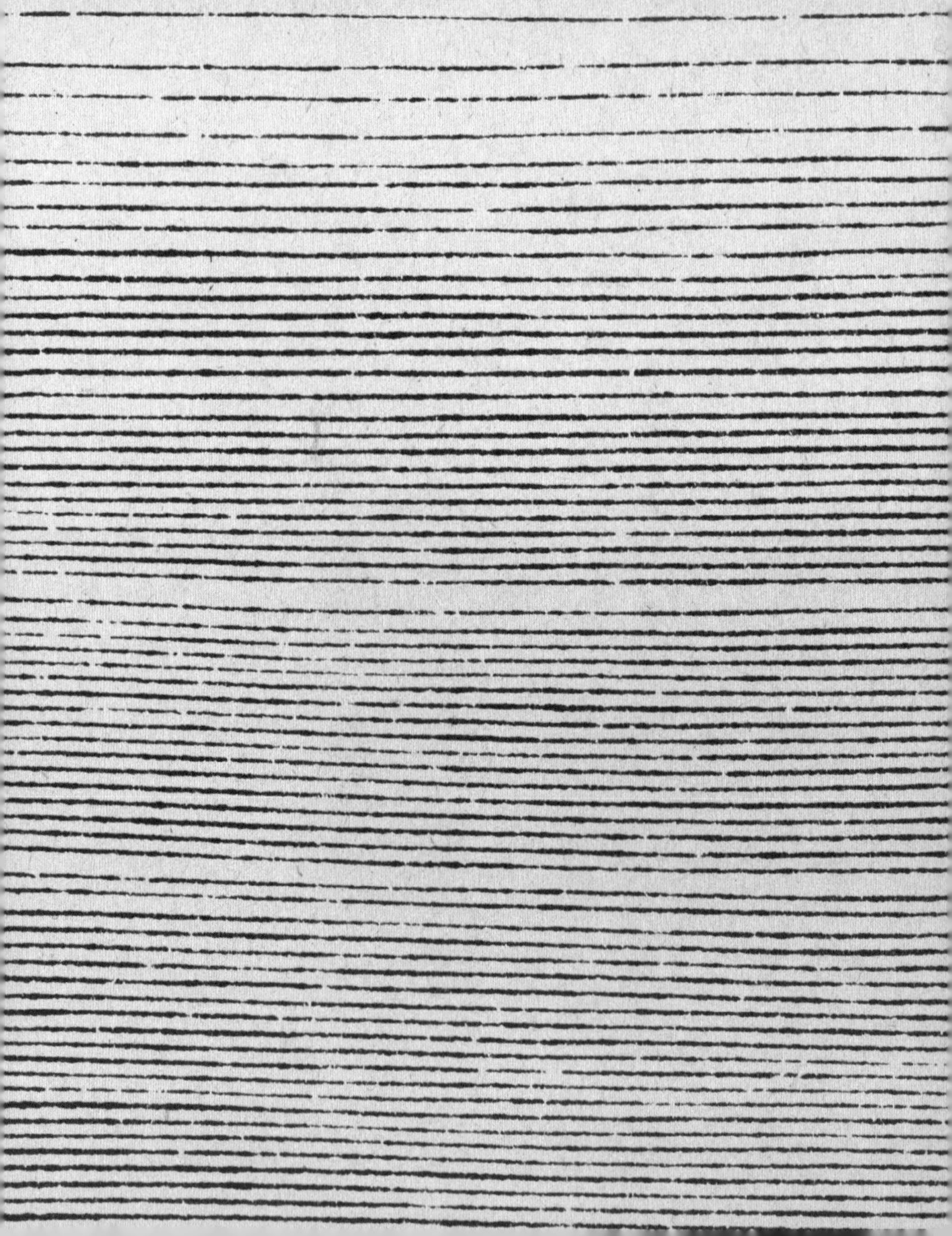

I think, if we're lucky, we spend our lives becoming more and more:

...live richly
with eyes open,
and heart, too.

GWENDOLYN BROOKS

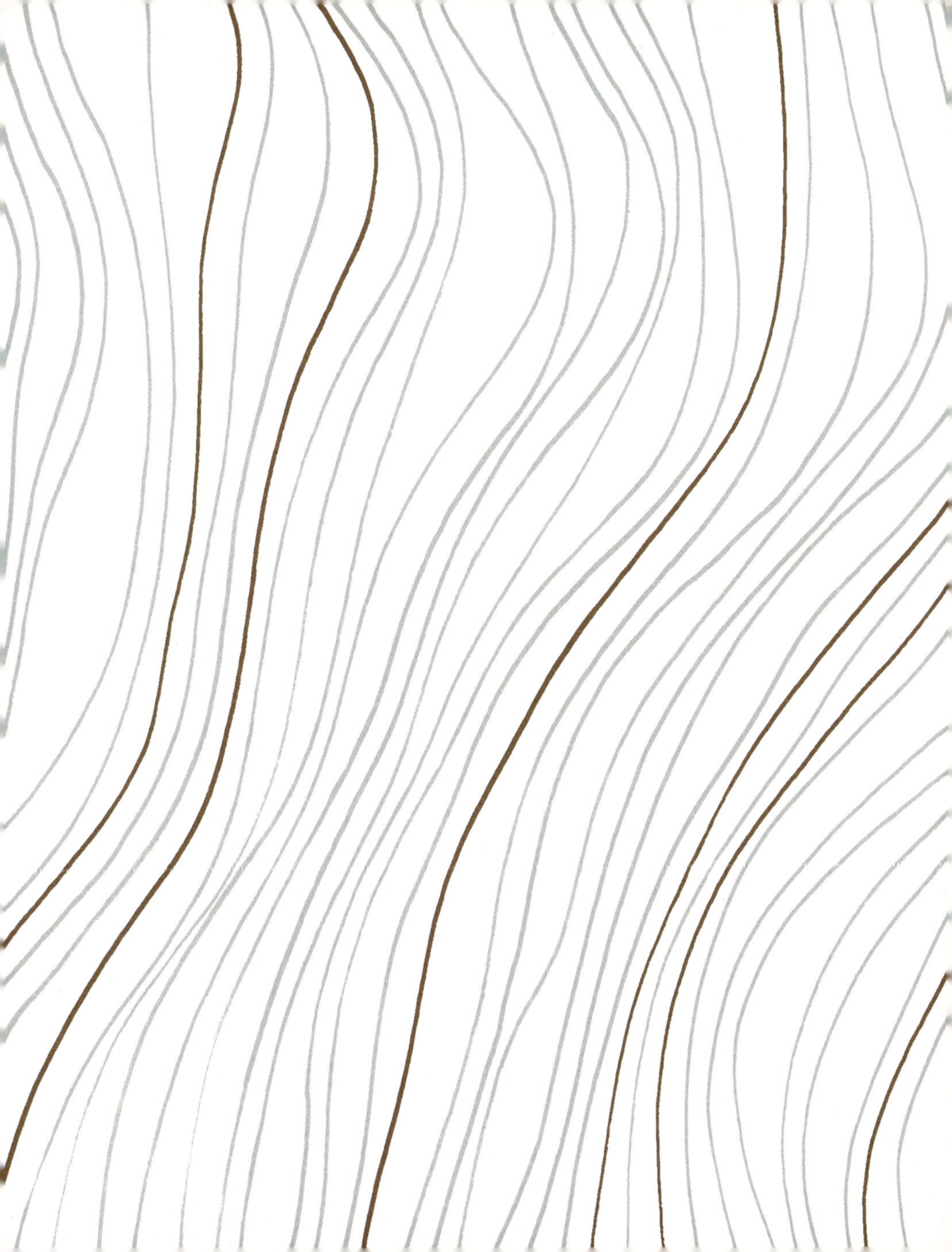

There are so many small, good things in an ordinary day. Here are just a few that bring me joy:

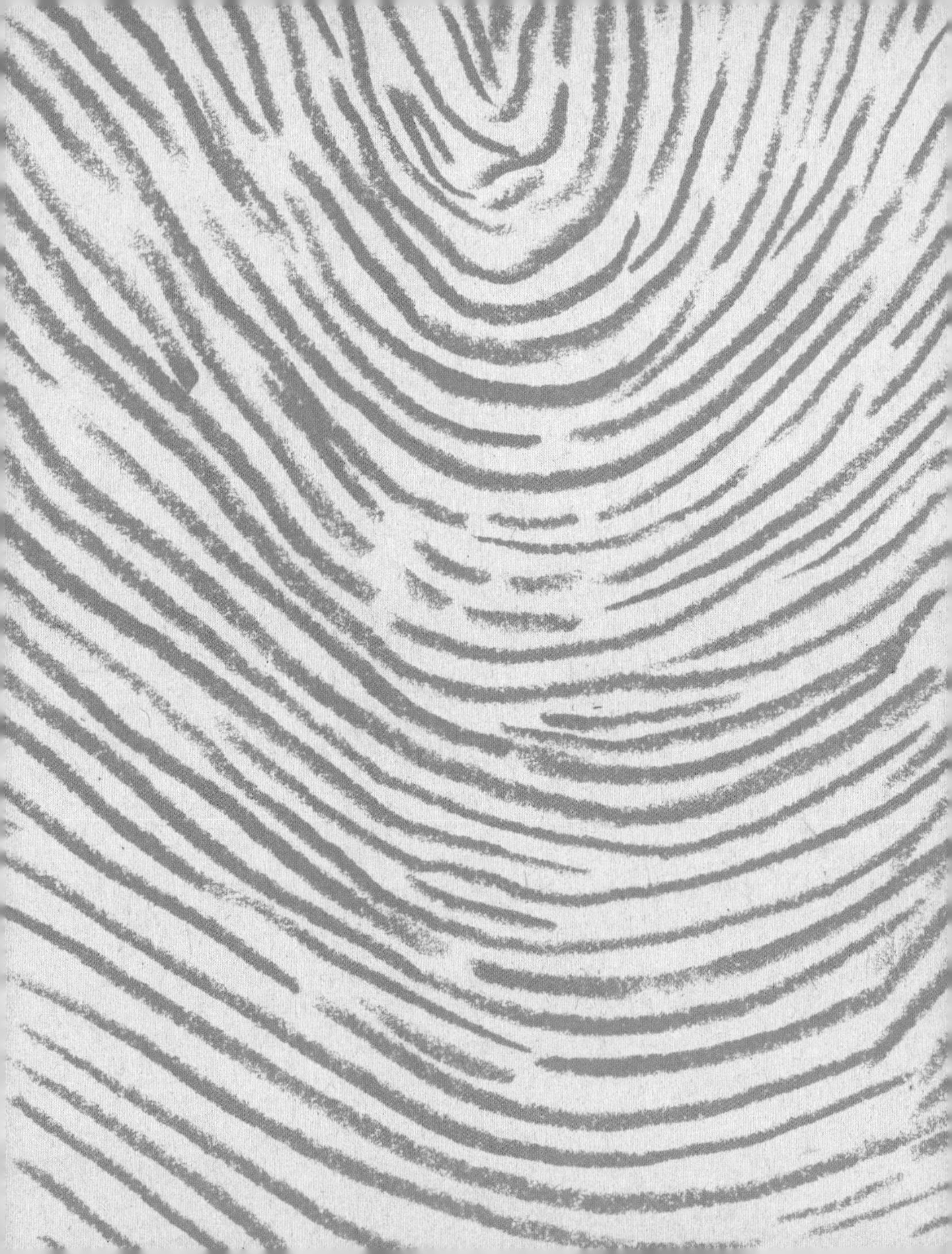

I THINK

_____

IS A LOT LESS IMPORTANT THAN WE BELIEVE.

AND

_____

IS A LOT MORE IMPORTANT THAN WE KNOW.

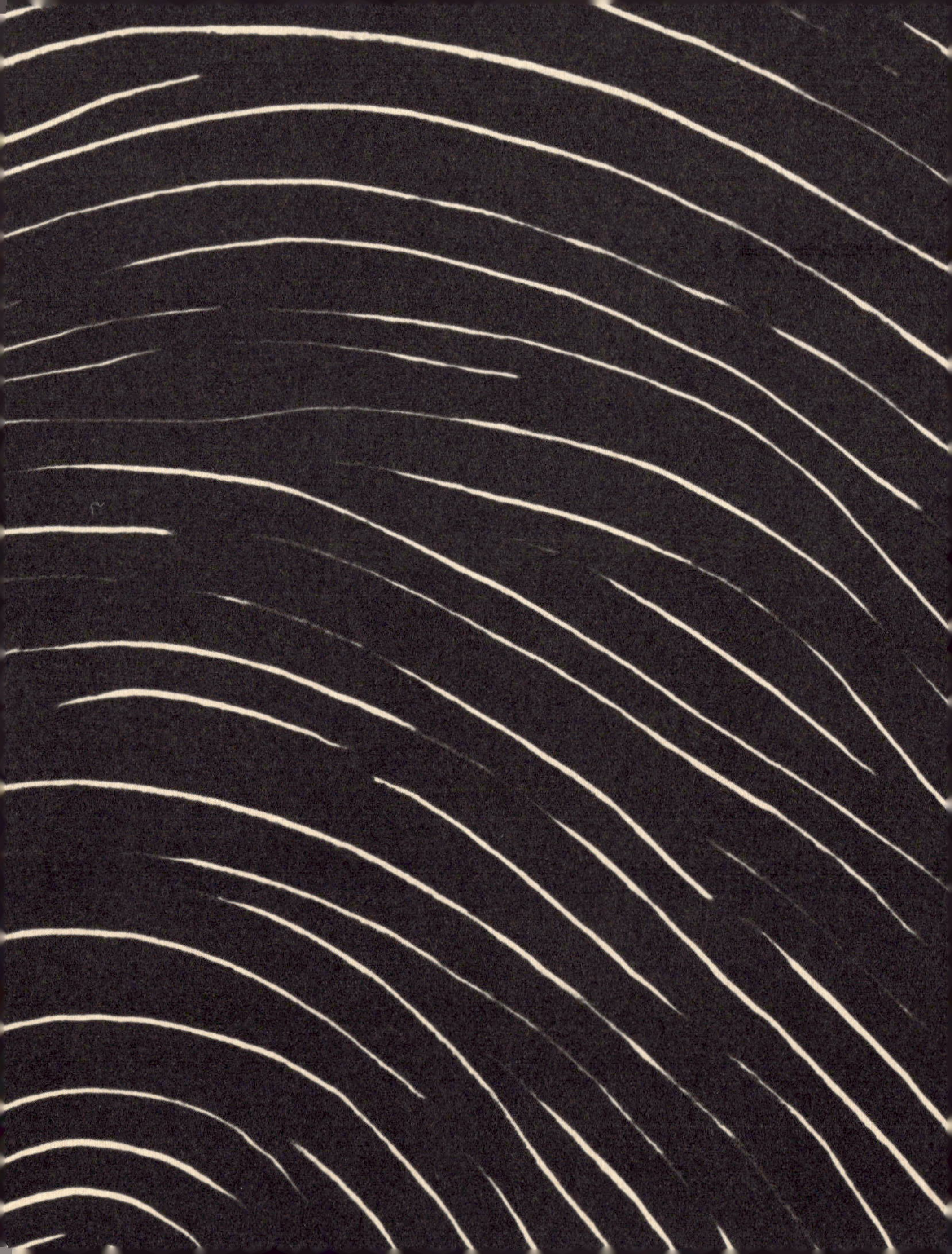

Despite our differences, in my experience most people want:

___

And most people appreciate:

___

It was worth it.
Love is worth it.

JEANETTE WINTERSON

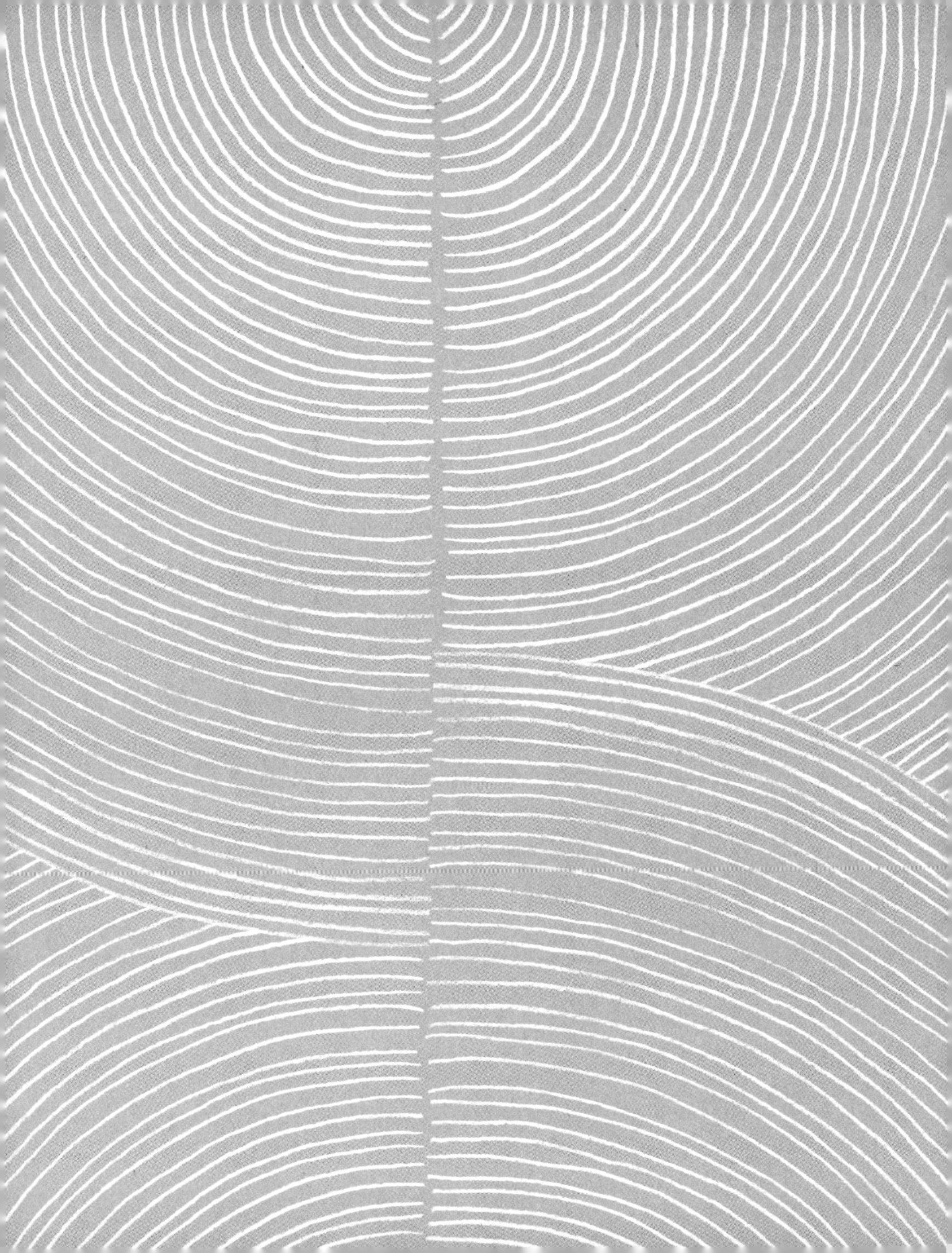

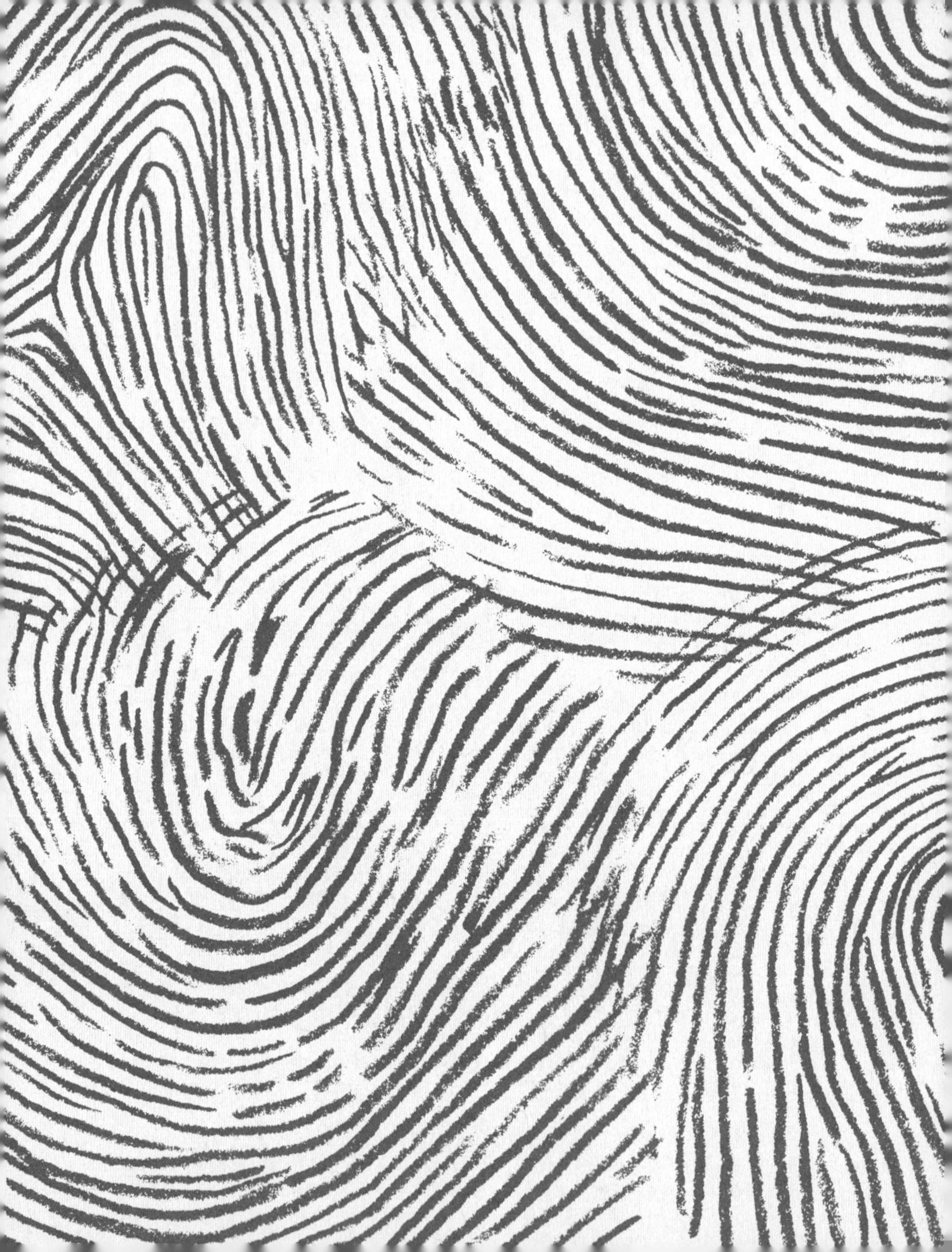

Love is such a complex word,
but this is how I define it:

And here's how I like to show it:

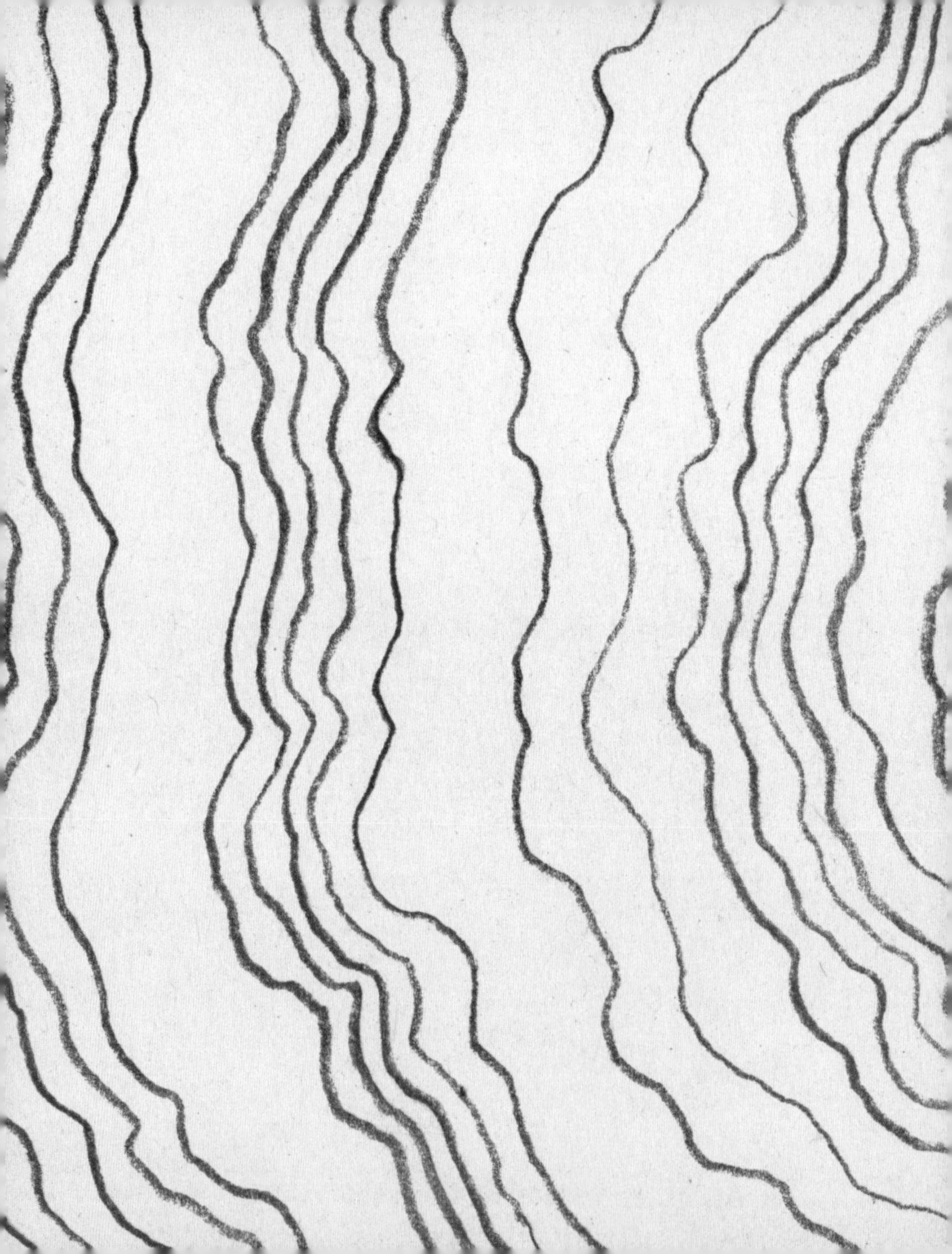

THE PEOPLE I LOVE HAVE TAUGHT ME SO MUCH.

THEY HAVE SHOWN ME
_____
_____

AND GIVEN ME
_____
_____

AND REMINDED ME
_____
_____

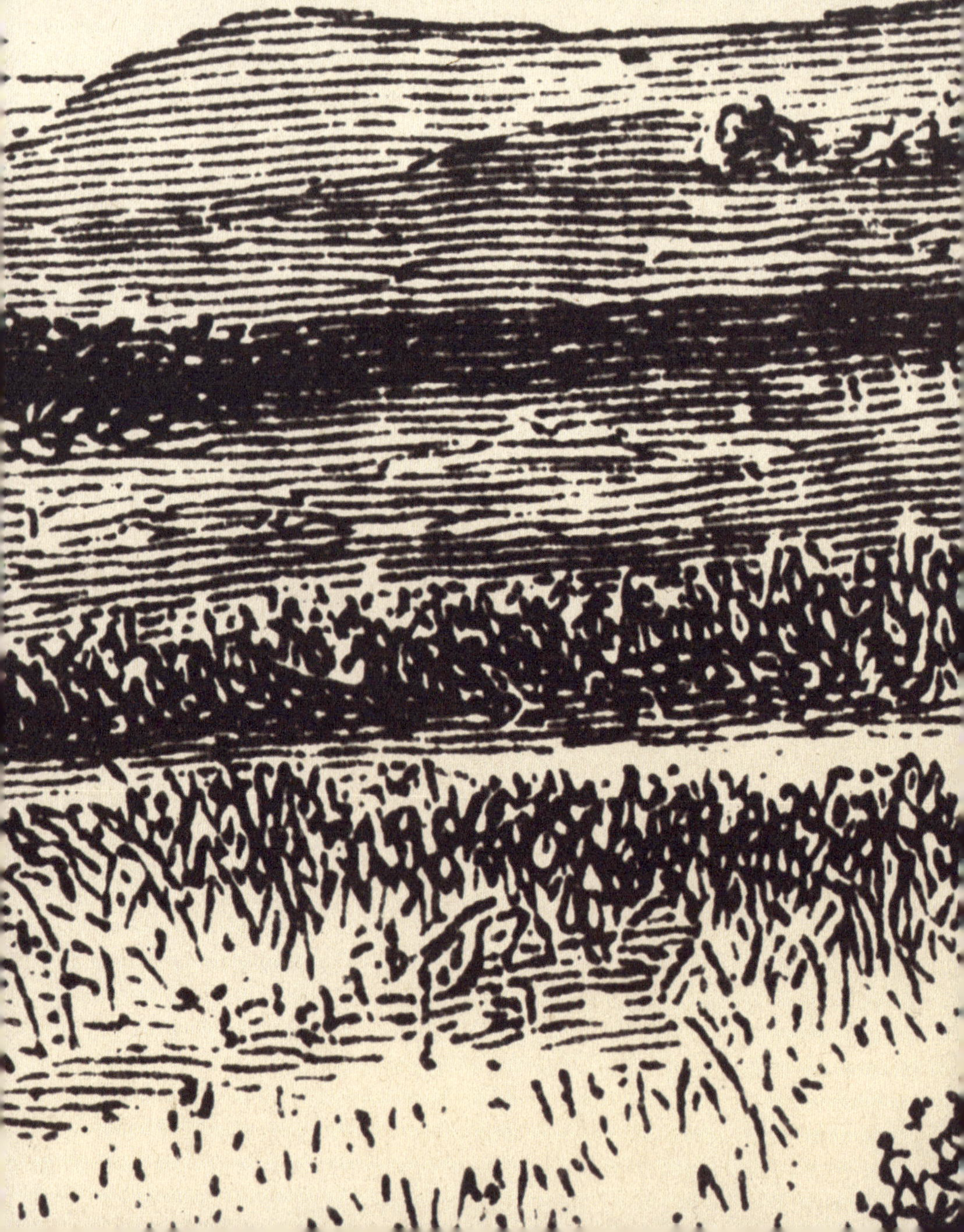

I think the most important thing
people can do for each other is:

We must discover
the joy of each other,
the joy of challenge,
the joy of growth.

MITSUGI SAOTOME

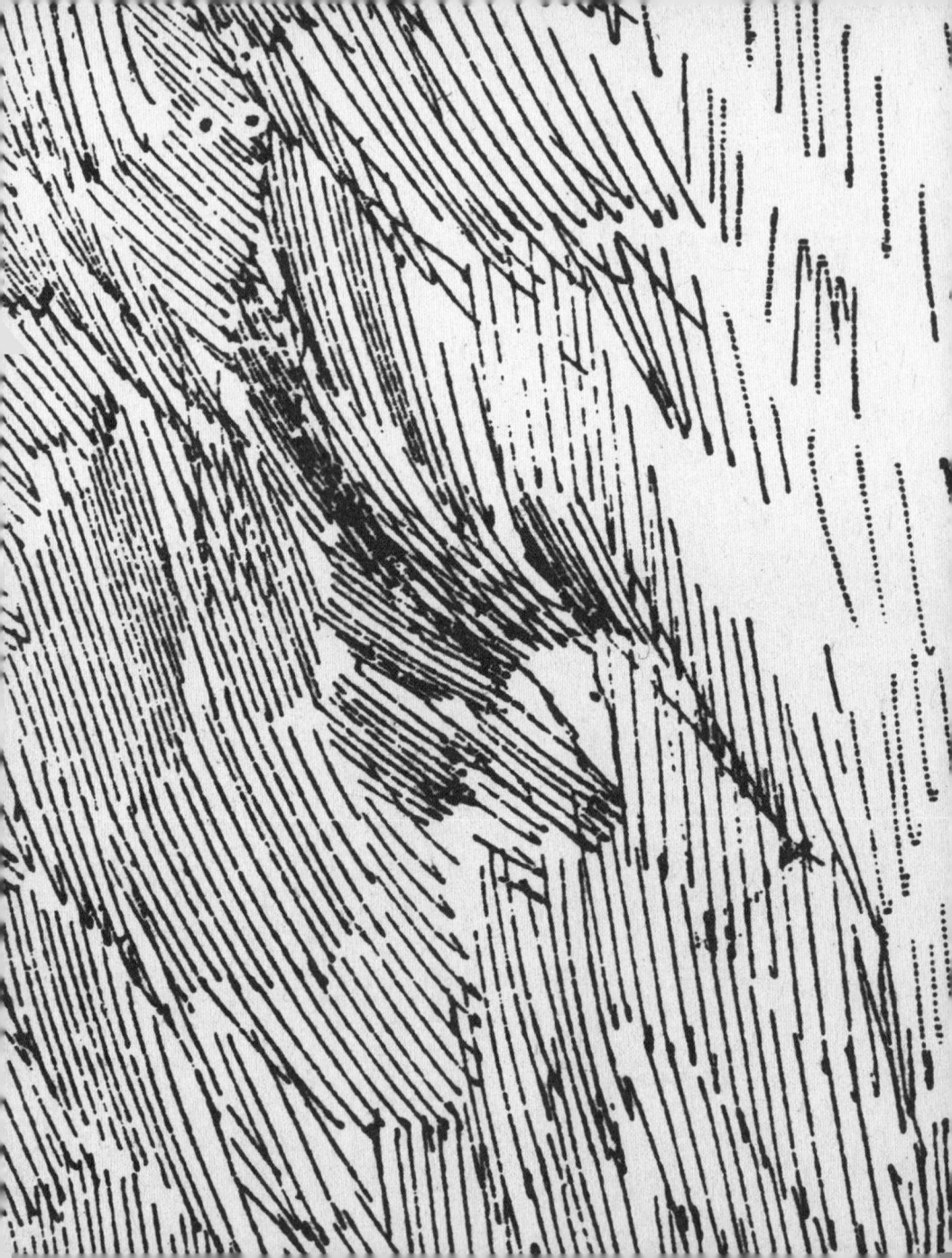

Life, no matter how beautiful, will always have its storms. I think that hardships have a way of showing us:

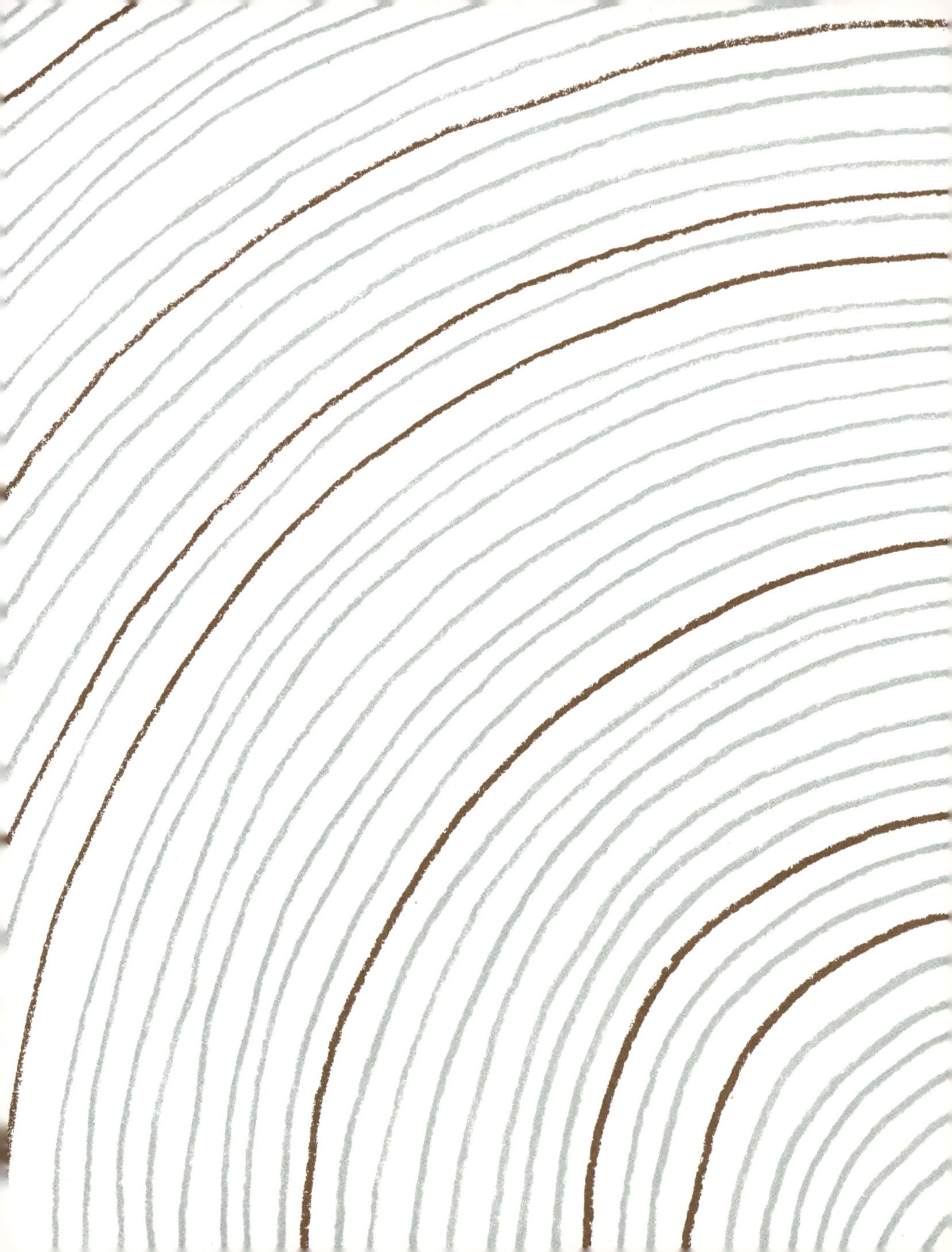

The years are full of surprises—things you don't expect, moments you can't plan for. These are some of the things I've relied on to get me through:

_____

_____

_____

_____

_____

_____

_____

_____

_____

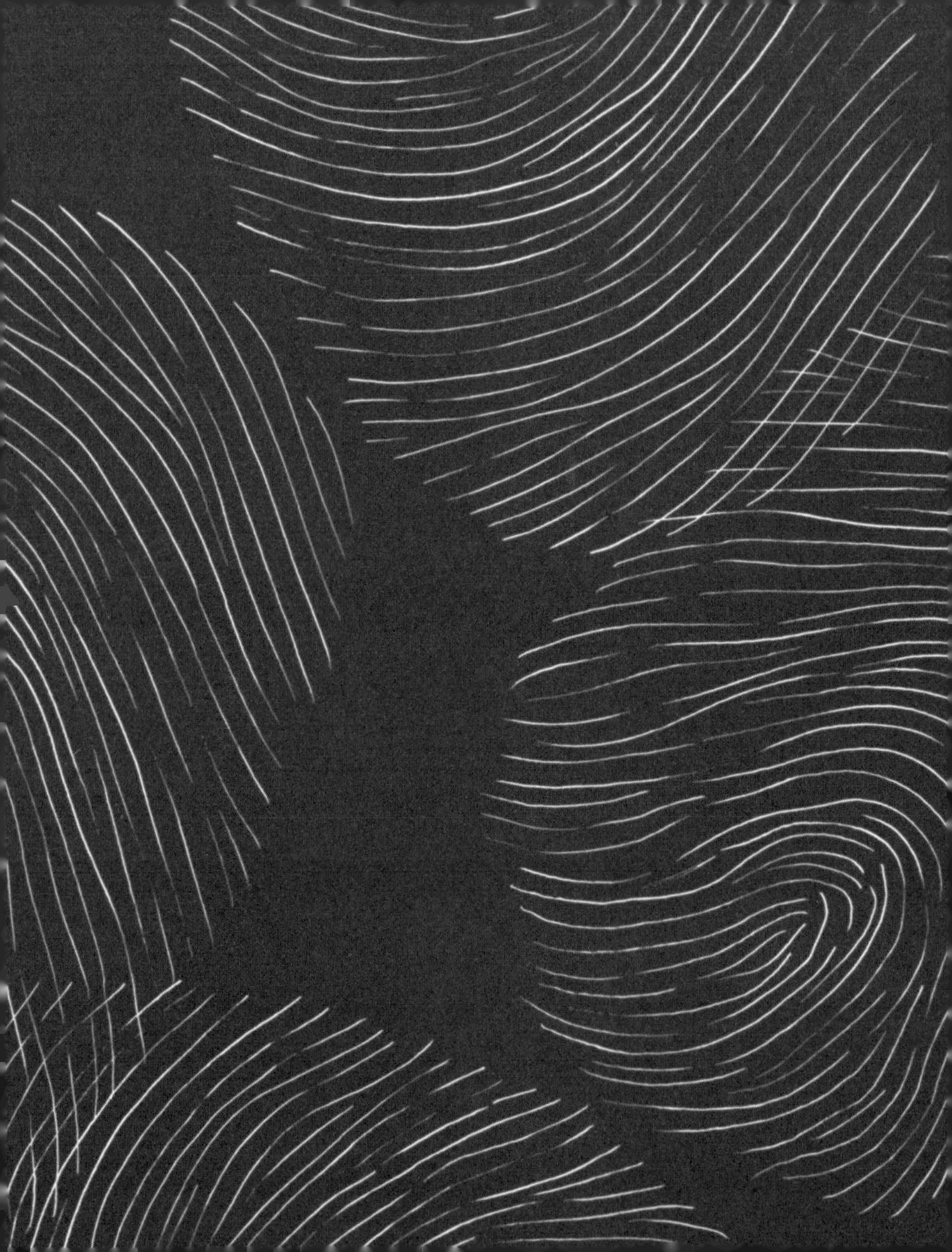

IF I COULD OFFER ONE PIECE OF ADVICE TO HELP SOMEONE THROUGH A DIFFICULT TIME, IT WOULD BE:

Life is not made up of minutes,
hours, days, weeks, months,
or years, but of moments.

SARAH BAN BREATHNACH

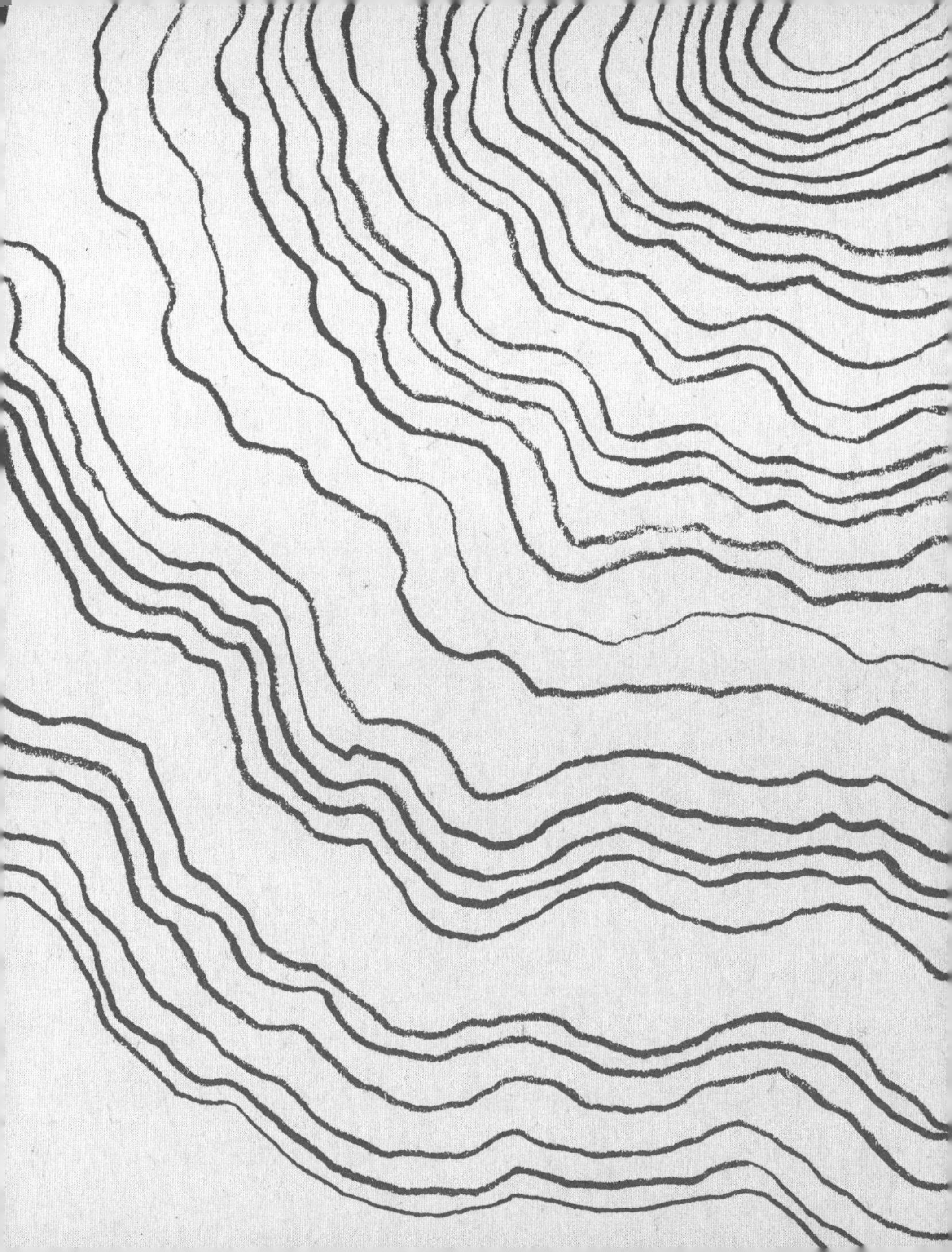

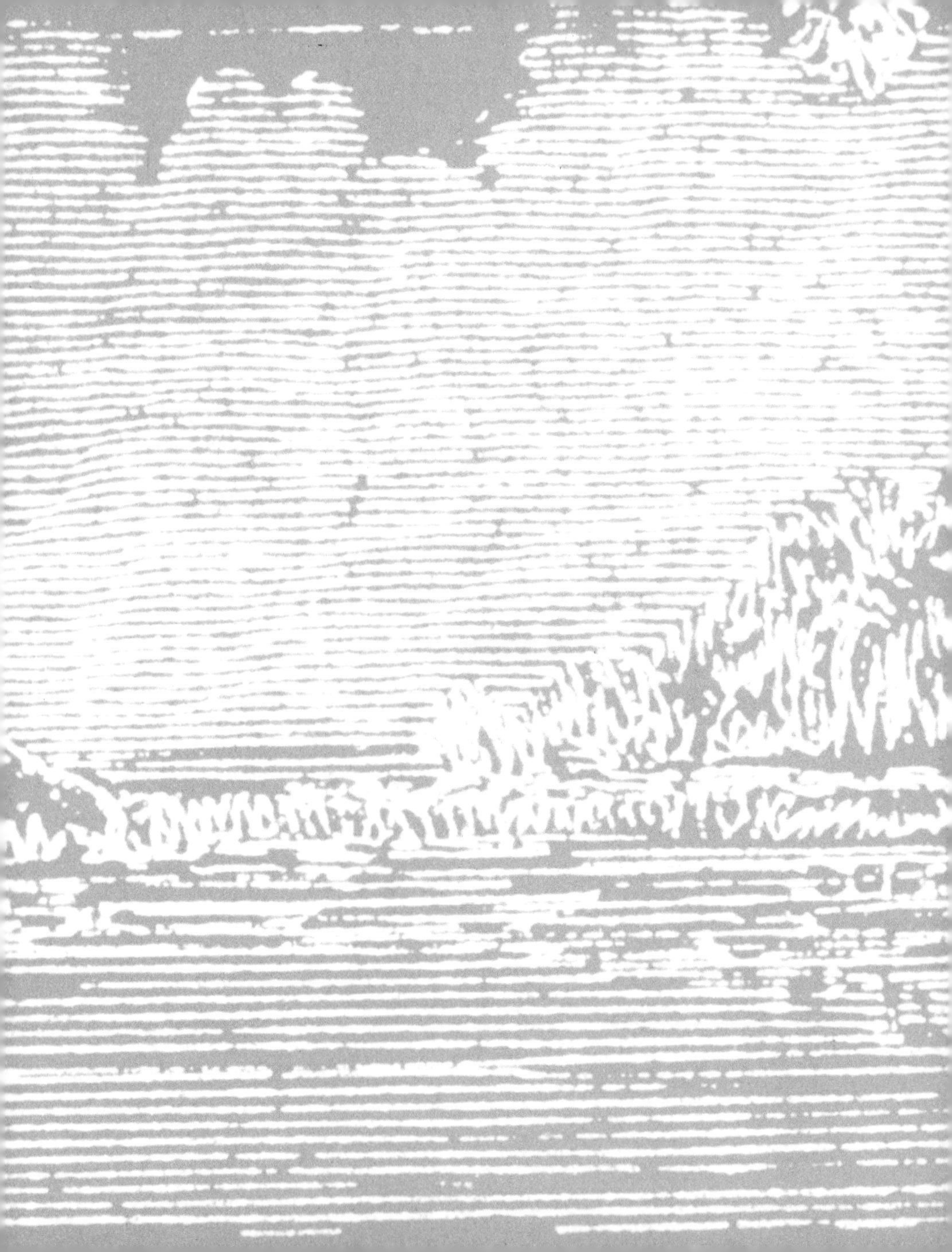

For me, these are the things that make moments matter:

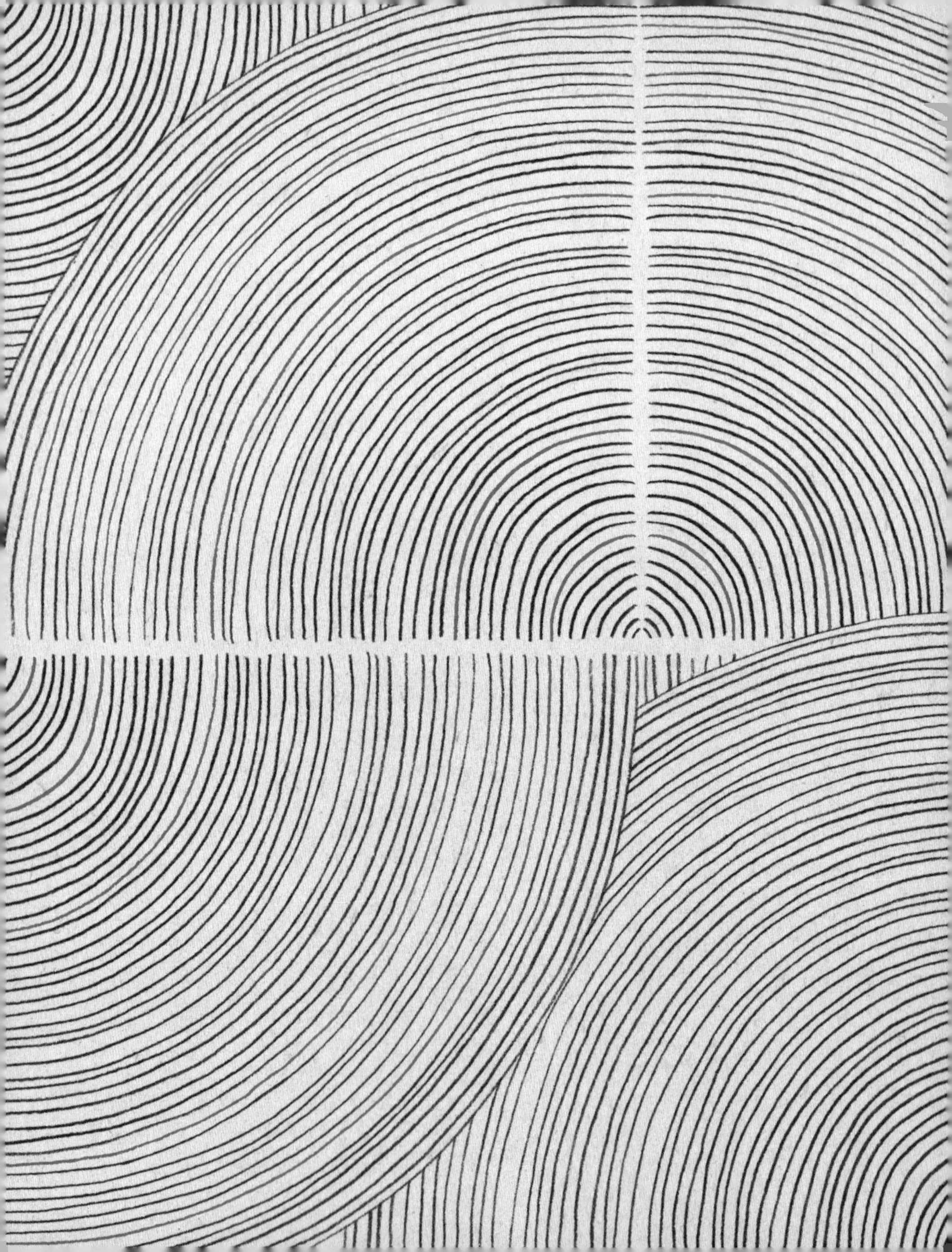

When I was younger, I would never have believed that:

_____

_____

_____

_____

But now, I've come to see:

_____

_____

_____

_____

_____

_____

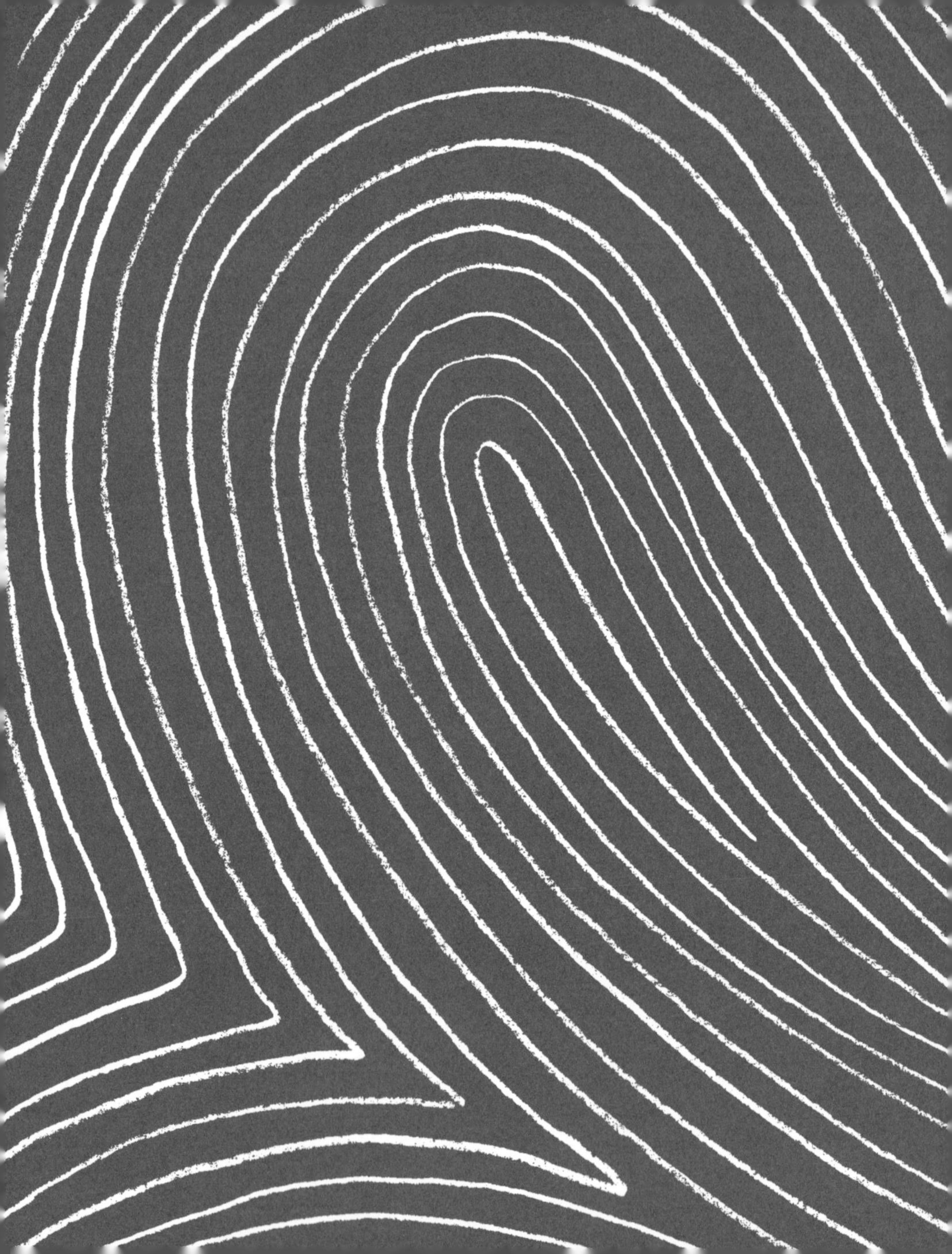

I am so grateful I have been able
to do these things in my lifetime:

It doesn't matter what you do... so long as you change something from the way it was before you touched it...

RAY BRADBURY

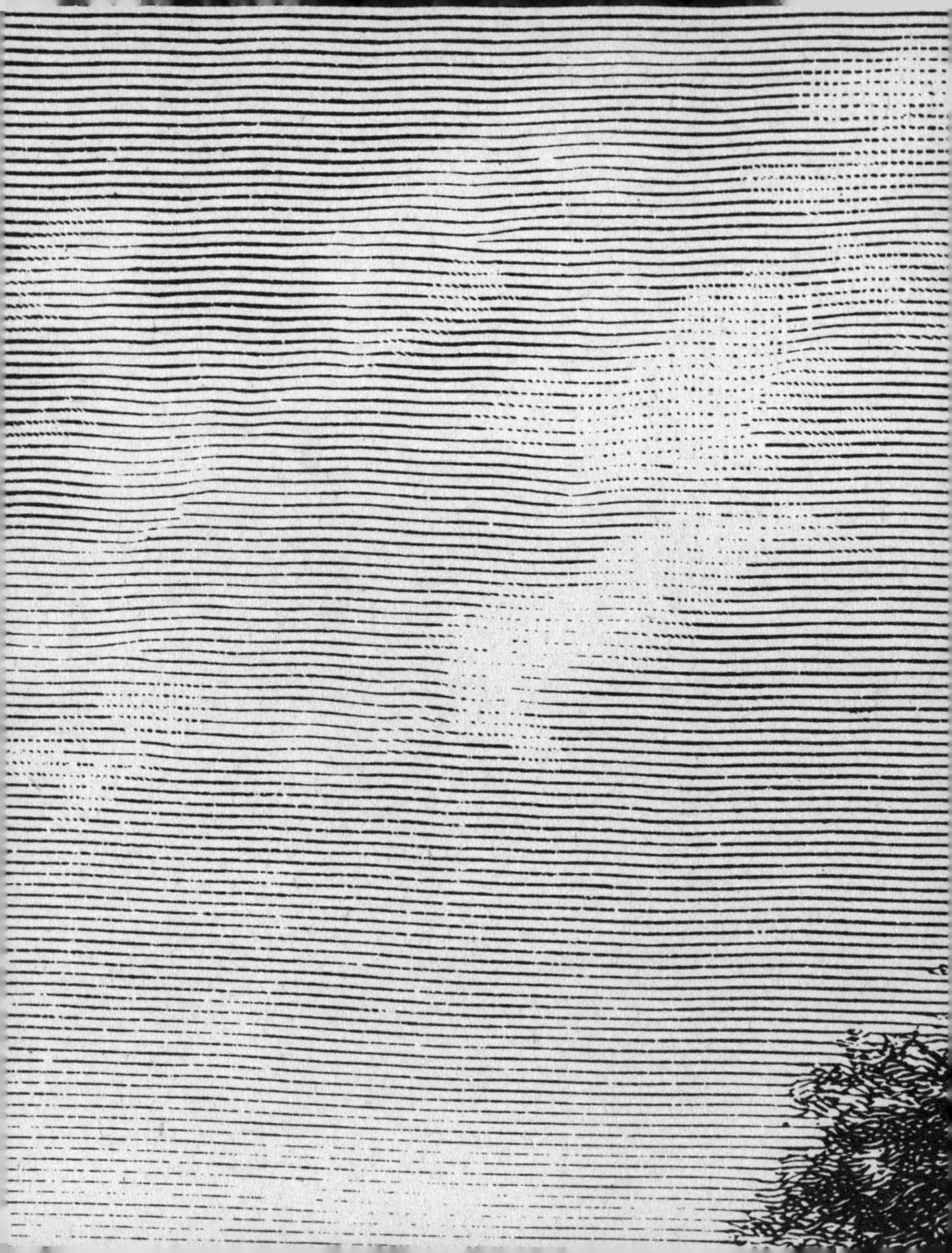

Looking back, I'm proud of the way I've:

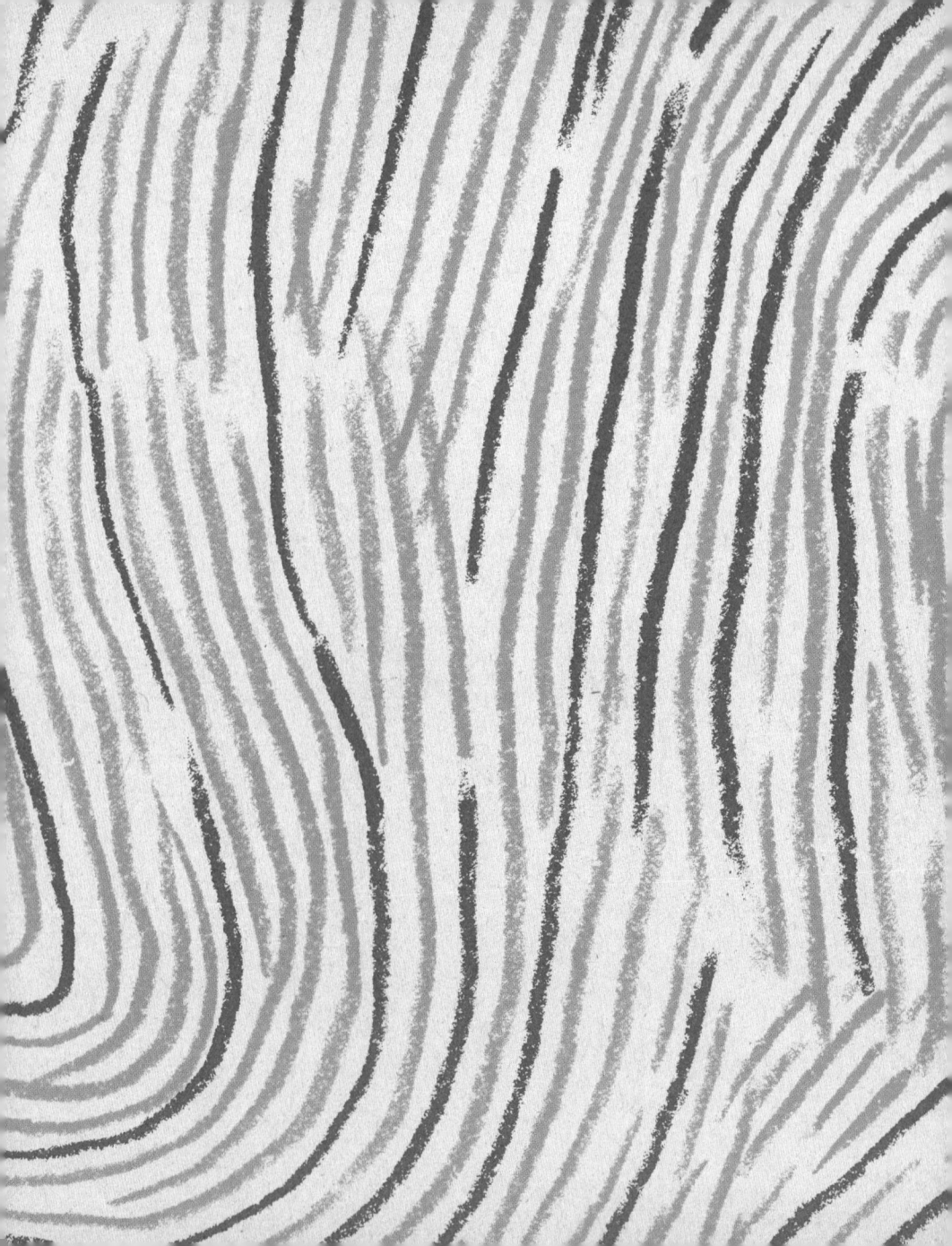

Most of all, I hope the people who know and love me remember me as:

Written by: M.H. Clark
Designed by: Jessica Phoenix
Edited by: Kristin Eade

Library of Congress Control Number: 2019957128 | ISBN: 978-1-970147-20-9

© 2021 by Compendium, Inc. All rights reserved. No part of this publication may be reproduced or transmitted in any form or by any means, electronic or mechanical, including photocopy, recording, or any storage and retrieval system now known or to be invented without written permission from the publisher. Contact: Compendium, Inc., 2815 Eastlake Avenue East, Suite 200, Seattle, WA 98102. *Most of All: A Legacy Book for Capturing the Stories of a Lifetime*; Compendium; live inspired; and the format, design, layout, and coloring used in this book are trademarks and/or trade dress of Compendium, Inc. This book may be ordered directly from the publisher, but please try your local bookstore first. Call us at 800.91.IDEAS, or come see our full line of inspiring products at live-inspired.com.

2nd printing. Printed in China with soy and metallic inks on FSC®-Mix certified paper.

Create meaningful moments with gifts that inspire.

CONNECT WITH US
live-inspired.com | sayhello@compendiuminc.com

@compendiumliveinspired
#compendiumliveinspired